MONEY MATTERS

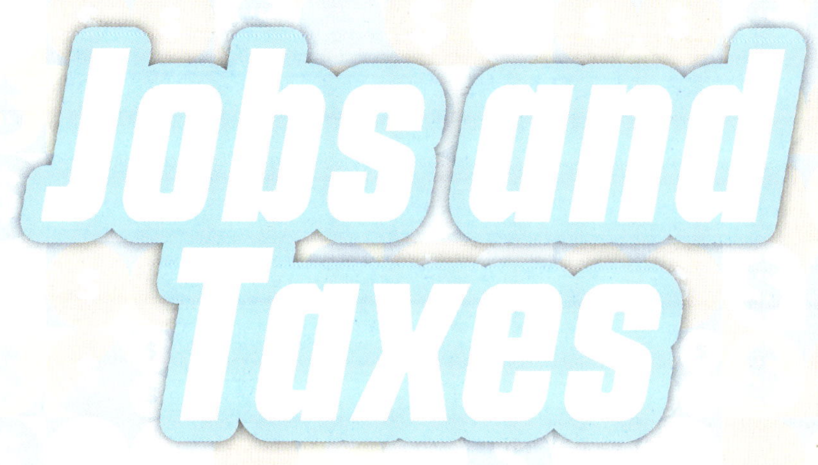

Jobs and Taxes

A Teen Guide to Earning Money

JENNIFER SANDERSON

Published in 2026 by **Cheriton Children's Books**
1 Bank Drive West, Shrewsbury, Shropshire, SY3 9DJ, UK

First Edition

Author: Jennifer Sanderson
Designer: Paul Myerscough
Editor: Kelly Short
Proofreader: Amy Strauss

Picture credits: Cover: Molibdenis Studio. Illustrations throughout by Molibdenis Studio. Inside: p4: Shutterstock/PeopleImages.com/Yuri A, p5: Shutterstock/Ipatov, p6: Shutterstock/N Universe, p7: Shutterstock/Robert Kneschke, p8: Shutterstock/Dragana Gordic, p9: Shutterstock/Quality Stock Arts, p11b: Shutterstock/BigPixel Photo, p11t: Shutterstock/Krakenimages.com, p12: Shutterstock/Quality Stock Arts, p13: Shutterstock/Andrey Popov, p14: Shutterstock/Gorynvd, p15: Shutterstock/Michael Jung, p17: Shutterstock/BearFotos, p18: Shutterstock/Gorodenkoff, p19: Shutterstock/Pics Five, pp20-21: Shutterstock/Vincent Nguyen, p22: Shutterstock/Prostock Studio, p23: Shutterstock/Gorodenkoff, p24: Shutterstock/PeopleImages.com/Yuri A, p25: Shutterstock/Chay Tee, p26: Shutterstock/Fizkes, p29: Shutterstock/Antonio Guillem, p30: Shutterstock/Ground Picture, p31: Shutterstock/Xavier Lorenzo, pp32-33: Shutterstock/I am Zews, p34: Shutterstock/Raushan Films, p35: Shutterstock/Africa Studio, p36: Shutterstock/Halfpoint, p37: Shutterstock/Lado, p38: Shutterstock/Prostock Studio, p39: Shutterstock/Phovoir, p41: Shutterstock/Bricolage, p42: Shutterstock/Ground Picture, p43: Shutterstock/Xmee, pp44-45: Shutterstock/PeopleImages.com/Yuri A.

Printed in China

Please visit our website,
www.cheritonchildrensbooks.com
to see more of our high-quality books.

Contents

CHAPTER 1

Why Money Matters

Money matters—it's at the heart of almost everything we do. We need money for food, clothing, a home, and to get around. Those are basic necessities or "needs." We also have "wants." These are life's luxuries—perhaps a great pair of sneakers, a vacation somewhere tropical, or a trip to the movies.

Needs Now, Needs Later

For now, your parents likely take care of your needs and even some of your wants. But as an adult, you'll take care of everything you need and want. You will need to earn money and manage the money you earn. You'll also have to pay taxes. Learning the skills to earn and manage your money now will help you do so in your adult life. And that's what we'll look at in this book.

When you have to pay for things yourself, you become more aware of the value of money and how much things cost.

When you are financially fit, saving for a great vacation is much easier.

Mastering Money

Developing your financial skills is a bit like going to the gym. Just as you may not be fit and strong when you start working out, the more you go, the easier it becomes. And you can soon see the benefits. By starting to grapple with simple finances now as a teenager, you'll be able to understand more complicated concepts as an adult. Money matters won't seem as overwhelming or scary either. You'll also feel more in control of your life and your future.

Fear Over Finances

Many teens say that they are pretty anxious about money, with around 54 percent stating that thinking about finances makes them worried. They say they do not feel that they are taught enough about money at school, and about 42 percent of teens say they have had no money-management classes in school. About 73 percent say they would take courses in money management if they were available. There is a big gap in financial education for teens. This book will help deal with that lack of education. It will give you the tools you need to feel confident about handling money and building your financial future.

Money Skills

With some simple financial skills, it is easy to get a grip on your money and feel in control of the sums going in and out. You can also develop those skills further, to help you make the most of your money. Some key financial skills include:

- Budgeting
- Saving
- Investing
- Earning
- Understanding taxes
- Managing debt
- Managing credit
- Setting financial goals
- Learning about insurance
- Getting to grips with risk and return

Earning and managing your money is a balancing act! We'll show you how to master it.

Learning about Financial Literacy

If you are someone who hasn't spent a lot of time thinking about finances so far, this book is as much for you as it is for someone who is very financially literate. Being financially literate means understanding basic things to do with money. That includes budgeting, saving, debt, credit, and investing. It covers managing risk, planning for the future, and knowing about tax. It also means being able to recognize when something is too financially good to be true! Everyone needs to be financially literate these days to navigate modern life and get the most from their money.

Making It Work for You

When you are financially literate, you can have a healthy and smart relationship with money. You understand how to make money work for you. With financial literacy you will not be alarmed or confused when people use the language of money. By the end of this book, we will have covered many key financial terms. We'll also have explained them, so you'll be well placed to handle any conversations about money in the future. Financial literacy gives you the tools you need to understand important information when you research money-related products.

The Key to Freedom

One of the greatest gifts that financial literacy will give you is a sense of control and freedom. When you are financially literate you understand the world of money and can make good decisions based on fact. You can choose how to spend your money. You can choose where to save your money. You may decide to borrow money at some point, perhaps by using a credit card or getting a loan. If you do, you'll be well equipped to understand the deals on offer and choose the best one for you. You will also be able to understand the language attached to lending, so you know exactly what you are getting yourself into.

You don't need to be great at math to master simple money skills and money doesn't have to be complicated. In this book, we'll try to make it as simple and easy to understand as possible. We'll take the mystery out of money and the fear away from finances. We'll show you how money can be exciting. We'll explain why it can give you freedom. And we'll show you how it can help you shape your future.

Teens and Money

Thinking about financial matters often scares teens and they feel unsure about how to manage their finances. That's mostly because it's not something they've really had to think about before. Teens who have grown up talking about money matters are generally more confident when it comes to managing their own finances. One way to build financial confidence is to talk to your parents and older siblings about how they manage their finances.

Money matters can seem confusing and overwhelming, but hopefully by the end of this book you'll understand more about earning money and paying your taxes.

Taking the First Step

In this book we will explore the skill of earning money. We'll also look at how, once you're earning money, you will at some point need to pay taxes. By earning your own money, you are taking steps to being financially independent from your parents. And there's also more than financial independence to be gained from earning your own money.

What Earning Money Can Do for You

Once you start working, it feels great to have your own money —and you'll gain important life skills too. One of the most useful is time management. This means planning how you use your time so you can finish everything you need to. With good time management, you can stay organized and still enjoy doing the things you love while keeping a job. Earning money also helps you become more self-reliant. And once you're confident managing your money, you'll likely feel more independent in other parts of your life as well.

Having a job and earning money teaches you important financial skills and also helps you learn to be independent.

If you go to college, you'll likely want to find work to help support yourself.

Even More Skills

Self-reliant teens are also confident teens. When you earn your own money, you become confident because you are in control. You control how much you spend and save. With this newfound confidence, you'll feel motivated to keep earning money, and this will keep you motivated to work hard throughout your life.

Working Toward Financial Freedom

We'll explore how to earn money now, while you are a teenager, and the benefits of doing so. We'll also take a look at how taxes work both now and in the future so that you understand them as an adult. Along the way, we'll cover advice from financial experts, so that you can learn to earn money and pay taxes like a pro. So, are you ready to make money work for you? Then let's get started.

Teens and Money

Research suggests that for every year a person works in their teens, their income rises significantly as a young adult in their 20s. This is largely because working teens learn and develop many new and important skills that they need as young adults. It gives them a head start on their peers who didn't work as teenagers.

CHAPTER 2

The Basics of Earning Money

Some parents give their teens an allowance. This is a great step toward helping them understand the value of money, but it isn't "earning" money. Earning money means you receive payment for work done, services completed, or goods bought and sold. You can also earn money from investments.

What the Law Says

When it comes to working, teens usually work on the weekends and perhaps one afternoon or evening a week. Full-time employees need a break, so teens fill the gaps to ensure businesses continue as normal. As a teen, work is governed by laws that say:

- No person under the age of 14 is allowed to work.
- 14- and 15-year-olds may work outside of school hours but not in manufacturing or hazardous jobs. Hazardous jobs include working in mining, logging, and operating heavy machinery.
- Teens cannot work more than three hours on a school day, including Fridays.
- They cannot work more than 18 hours a week when schools are in session.
- They cannot work before 7am or after 7pm (except between June 1 and Labor day, when evening shifts can end at 9pm).
- Teens can work up to 8 hours a day and 40 hours a week in school breaks.
- 16- and 17-year-olds can work unlimited hours in any non-hazardous job.

States can have their own extra laws. For example, in some states, teenagers must have a valid work permit. Often, parents must give their consent for the permit to be issued. If the state law is different from the federal law, the law that is more protective over the teenager is the one that must be followed.

If you do work while studying, make sure you get enough rest time. Doing too much will leave you exhausted.

At a Minimum

Just as there are laws to protect teens, there is also a minimum wage that employers must pay their workers. In 1938, the minimum wage was just 25 cents but, fortunately, this has increased! In 2025, the minimum wage was $7.25 per hour. There is also a youth minimum wage that those under 20 years old can be paid during their first 90 days of work. In 2025, that figure was $4.25 an hour.

Teens and Money

Most teens will only earn the minimum youth wage when they first start working. While that can be disappointing, it's important to realize that everyone has to start somewhere. It's also worth remembering that being a working teen has many more benefits than the money earned. Working teens develop important skills to help them navigate life.

Having a part-time job is a great way to gain financial freedom as a teen.

What Type of Work?

If you choose to earn money by finding a job, you might wonder what work is best suited to teens. One popular option for teens is retail, offering opportunities in grocery stores, pharmacies, clothing stores, and more. If you have a particular interest or hobby, you can make good use of it by working in stores that match that interest or hobby. For example, if you like sports, you might work well at a sporting goods store. Your knowledge can help you assist customers and sell products to them more confidently. You usually earn reliable pay and get regular shifts in retail work, too.

Could You Work in Retail?

In retail, you might stock shelves or help keep the store tidy. If you're a good communicator, you could work with customers—using quick thinking and problem solving to handle any issues. Some teens work as cashiers at checkouts. In that role, being alert and responsible is important. Having strong math skills helps too, because you'll be dealing with payments and banking cards.

Working with Food

Many teens find jobs in food services. That might be restaurants, fast-food outlets, and concession stands. Tasks might range from taking orders to flipping burgers. These roles depend on teamwork and strong social and communication skills. They help you learn to work well with others and keep customers happy.

Working on a shop floor is not for everyone. If you are organized and pay attention to detail, working in a warehouse could suit you.

Any new job will require some training, especially if you need to learn how a new computer program works. Once you learn one program, any new one won't be as difficult to master.

Mastering Money

Everyone starting a new job should be given an employment contract. As well as listing the job you'll be doing, the contract should cover wages and hours. Before accepting the job, it's important to understand the role and expectations. To do this, you should also be able to answer these questions:

- How will I be paid? Will I need a bank account or will I be paid in cash?
- How will I deal with the hours? What would a typical week look like?
- Will I be given time off during test and exam periods?
- Will I be able to get to work easily or will I have to rely on a parent or older sibling for transportation?

Working with younger children gives teens a chance to be mentors, helping and guiding others.

Paid for Something You Are Good At

If retail or the food services industry is not for you, that doesn't mean you won't find work. There are many jobs for teens in which they are paid for a service. These roles are often based on your personal skills and interests. A big benefit is that you'll likely enjoy the work. But keep in mind that service jobs may not offer regular hours like shift work. For many teens, that flexibility is a good thing—it leaves more time for school and fun.

Like Working with Children?

If you enjoy spending time with children, consider doing babysitting, working as a camp counselor, or helping at a daycare. You'll need to be patient, responsible, and caring. It's also smart to get a first aid certification, so you're ready to help if an emergency happens.

If you're strong in a subject like math, you could tutor younger students. Or if you're more into music or sports, you could teach basic skills on an instrument or help coach a youth team. Tutoring and coaching are both meaningful jobs—you get to help someone grow and improve. It also looks great on college or job applications, especially if you're thinking about a career in teaching.

Using Your Skills

Some teens have hobbies that can turn into money-making jobs. Love gardening? Try lawn care or landscaping. You might start with mowing or weeding, and learn more as you go. Enjoy swimming and being outdoors? Lifeguarding could be a great fit. You'll need training and a first aid certificate, but the skills you learn will last a lifetime. Just remember, this kind of work is seasonal. You'll need to save money for the times when work slows down.

Teens and Money

In a survey of parents with working teens, 76 percent said having a job improved their teen's money skills. Seventy percent said it boosted self-esteem, and 63 percent saw better time-management skills in their children. Teens also said that they felt they had learned important life skills like leadership, creativity, and how to communicate well.

If you like working outside, why not try your hand at gardening? It can be a great way to make money during the spring and summer.

Get Financially Fit:

Make Money like a Pro

Expert Tips!

Having a job is a great way to earn money but what if you want something more? What if you want to be your own boss—is that even possible as a teenager? YES it is! You can be an entrepreneur. If you decide to set up your own business, here are a few key pointers from experts who have done just that.

Spot Opportunities

The first step to being an entrepreneur is spotting a gap in the market, which means thinking of something that people need or want that isn't readily available. It also means that you realize that something could become popular, and you take the risk to make that happen.

Think Outside of the Box

Once you identify a gap in the market, you need to find a solution to fill that gap. And that's not just any old solution—it needs to be an innovative one. Something that's innovative has never been done before. It is brand new and creative.

Some teens start businesses as painters and decorators.

Take a Risk

The hardest part of being an entrepreneur is taking the risk. A risk means you do something even though you may not get the outcome you desire. This is where your grit and determination come in: Not all risks pay off so you need to be prepared for that. If at first you don't succeed, try again. If the risk pays off, it'll definitely be worth it.

Manage Your Success

Once everything is up and running, you need to manage your business. You'll have to invest some money to start it off. That might mean using your savings, if you have them. It could also mean taking a loan from your parents. Remember, a loan needs to be paid back, so you'll need to plan your budget carefully. And of course, you can't just sit back and relax! You need to keep at it to make sure your business grows and does well.

Think like an Entrepreneur

Be curious—people with successful businesses want to grow or learn. They ask questions and see learning as an opportunity to grow. Think critically—that means analyzing things, evaluating them, and interpreting information. Be ready to problem-solve too. Entrepreneurs think outside of the box. Be determined—it won't always be easy, so dig in and keep on going. If you talk to any person who has run their own business, they will tell you that they had to overcome many challenges.

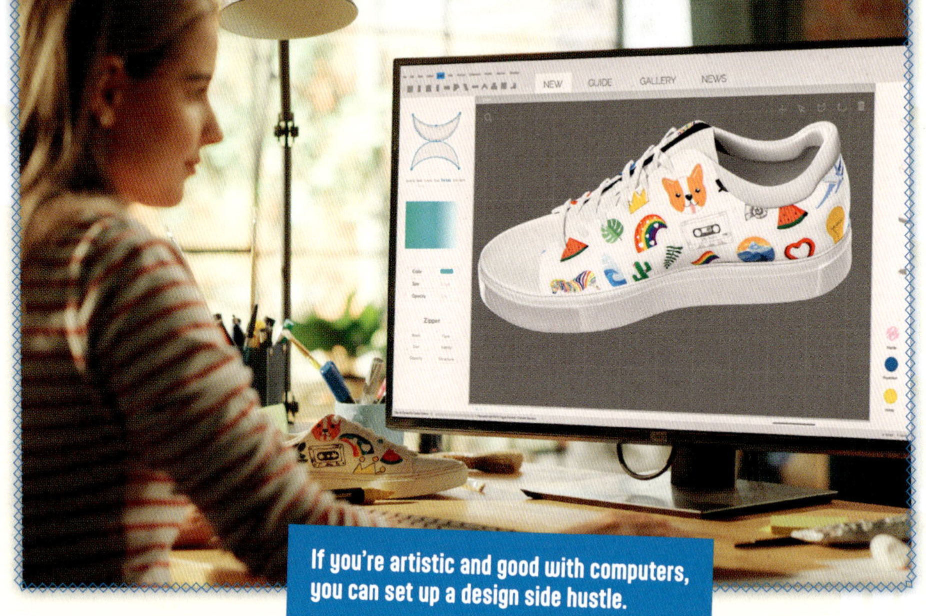

If you're artistic and good with computers, you can set up a design side hustle.

Buy and Sell

Another way to earn money is by buying and selling goods. To do this, you'll need to start with some money. This is known as your capital. Using your capital, you'd buy something, say for $10, and sell it for more, say $15. This means that you make $5 for every item that you sell. That $5 is called your profit.

You can reinvest your profit in more goods. You could also make a product and sell it at a profit.

Making Money Online

As a teen, you probably spend a lot of time online. That means you likely have better tech skills than people who didn't grow up with the Internet. One way to earn money is to use these tech skills to create content. You could create your own content and build up a following. With a large following, you'll draw in companies that want to sponsor or advertise on your content.

With a bit of help from an adult, you can start to understand how the stock market works.

Investing Your Money

If you are money-smart, you'll want to start investing as soon as possible. By investing in your teens, your money has a long time to grow. What may seem like a small amount now, will become a large amount when you're an adult. You'll then have the money you need to pay for things such as a car or a down payment on a home. You can invest in several ways:

- **A bank account with a high interest rate:** This means that your money will grow without you having to do anything.
- **Bonds:** These are loans that investors make to a company. The borrower pays you interest over a set period of time.
- **Stocks:** These are shares in a company. You buy a share and when the company does well, you're paid money.
- **Mutual funds:** In these funds, money is pooled together from other investors to buy stocks and bonds.
- **Exchange Traded Funds (ETFs):** This is a package of stocks. Instead of picking several individual stocks, you invest in several at the same time.

We'll look at long-term investing later on too, so make sure you keep reading.

Mastering Money

The stock market is like an online store, but instead of buying goods, you are buying a share in companies. You can buy and sell your shares at any time so by investing in shares, you'll learn to live with the highs and lows of making and losing money. You'll also learn patience because investing in the stock market is not a quick fix. Although you'll need to be 18 to set up your own stock market account, you could ask a parent or guardian to help you set up a custodial account. They would manage the account until you are 18.

Earning Money Made Easy

To remind you why it's a great idea to start earning money now as a teenager and how you can do it, let's take a another look at everything we covered in chapter 2.

Check What the Law Says

There are rules about how much work a teen can do, and the type of work too. Check out any job you're interested in to make sure it fits with those regulations.

Working to Earn

Earning money by having a job in retail or the food services industry is a great way for teens to earn money. There are different jobs, depending on your skills and what you like to do.

Offer a Service

Teens can earn while doing the things they enjoy by selling their services, from babysitting to lifeguarding. These jobs are great for honing skills and doing things you like. On the one hand, they offer flexibility when it comes to working hours. But on the other, the work may be seasonal. This means you'll need to be good at budgeting and saving.

Making a Profit

Buying or making goods and selling them at a profit is a great way to earn money. While you may not make a huge profit, it's a good way to grow your initial investment.

Be an Entrepreneur

You can set up your own business as a teen. By being smart and coming up with an innovative idea, the earning potential for teen entrepreneurs is high.

You're Not Too Young to Invest

You may not be able to be a fully-fledged stock broker until you're 18. However, with the help of an adult you can invest your money wisely. There are several different options, so check them out really carefully. Then decide what is best for you.

CHAPTER 3

How to Pay Taxes

Everyone in the country has civic responsibilities. These are duties we have as citizens—for example, following the law and voting when we're old enough. Once you start earning money, paying taxes becomes one of your responsibilities too.

What Are Taxes?

Taxes are money paid to the government. People who earn money must pay taxes by law. If you don't, you could face a fine—or worse, go to jail.

In the United States, we pay federal, state, and local taxes. Federal taxes help fund national programs. They include military defense, public education, and healthcare for people in need. They also include unemployment benefits and medical research. They help pay pensions for veterans and government workers too.

State and local taxes are used for things closer to home—like schools, roads, public buses, police, and fire departments. Each city and state decides what its own tax money pays for, so this can vary a lot depending on where you live.

Did you know that the yellow school buses students ride are often funded by both state and local tax dollars?

If you buy clothes in Louisiana, you'll pay an incredible 10.12 percent combined state and local sales tax.

Taxes When You Shop

When you shop, you may notice extra money added at checkout. That's sales tax—a tax on things you buy in stores. It's usually a percentage of the item's price. Everyone pays the same rate, no matter how much they earn. Sales tax differs between states —and even cities. Some items are exempt. For example, in New York, clothing and footwear under $110 per item are exempt from the 4 percent state sales tax. Five states—Oregon, Montana, Delaware, Alaska, and New Hampshire—don't have sales tax. Several states hold sales tax holidays. During them, there are temporary exemptions on items like school supplies or clothing. These typically last a few days and take place during shopping peaks, such as back-to-school season.

Mastering Money

Before you go to the checkout, it's a good idea to have a rough idea of how much the sales tax will be. Let's take a look at how to calculate the sales tax on an item.

- First, find out the sales tax as a percentage. Convert that percentage to a decimal. For example, 8 percent sales tax is written as 0.08.
- Multiply the price of your item by the sales tax as a decimal to figure out how much tax needs to be added. For example, if the item costs $25, your calculation is 25 x 0.08 = 2.
- Add the answer from step 2 to your item's price: 25+2 = 27.
- You will pay $27 for the item.

Understanding Income Tax

There is one kind of tax that affects almost every person who earns money—even teens—and that's income tax. As the name suggests, this tax is money paid to the government based on how much you earn. Most people pay federal income tax. Some states also charge state income tax on top of that. When you get a paycheck, income tax is usually taken off before you even see it. This is called a deduction. Your employer takes a portion of your earnings and sends it straight to the government.

So, How Much Do You Pay?

The amount of income tax you pay depends on how much you earn. The United States uses a system called progressive tax. That means people who earn more pay a higher percentage. The government splits income into levels called tax brackets. Each bracket has its own tax rate. As your income goes up, the part of your earnings in the next bracket gets taxed at a higher rate. But you only pay the higher rate on the money in that bracket—not on all of your income. So, if part of your income is in a lower bracket, it's taxed at the lower rate.

A progressive tax system does not depend on age. A teen who develops an app and sells subscriptions to it may earn more money than a 20-year-old working as a barista, and so will pay more income tax.

If you earn money as a self-employed content creator, you will need to pay income tax if you reach the threshold.

Earning a Little, Earning a Lot

To make income tax a little fairer and to help those who don't earn a lot, the government sets a threshold that people have to earn before they must pay taxes. In 2025, the threshold was $13,850. This means that a teenager who worked for someone and earned less than $13,850 will not owe taxes. If they earned more than the threshold amount, they would pay tax on the amount that is above the threshold. There is also a threshold on the amount of money made from interest on investments or dividends from stocks and shares. In 2025, that was $1,250.

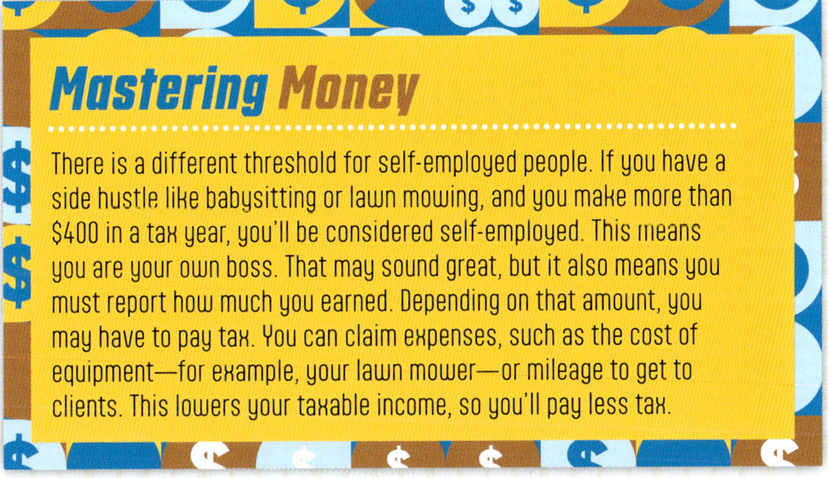

Mastering Money

There is a different threshold for self-employed people. If you have a side hustle like babysitting or lawn mowing, and you make more than $400 in a tax year, you'll be considered self-employed. This means you are your own boss. That may sound great, but it also means you must report how much you earned. Depending on that amount, you may have to pay tax. You can claim expenses, such as the cost of equipment—for example, your lawn mower—or mileage to get to clients. This lowers your taxable income, so you'll pay less tax.

Taxes and More Taxes

Income tax isn't the only deduction from your paycheck. The IRS also takes out money for Social Security and Medicare. You may not see the benefits now, but one day you might need them, so it's good to understand how they work.

Paying Social Security

The Social Security program started in 1935. The first payment was made to Ida M. Fuller—for just $22.54. Today, the program is much bigger. In 2024, more than 72 million Americans got Social Security benefits.

Social Security is run by the Federal government through the Social Security Administration (SSA). Most people think of it as retirement money, but it also helps people who are disabled and unable to work.

You can start getting Social Security at age 65, but you'll get more each month if you wait until age 70. The amount you receive depends on your average monthly income over your 35 highest-earning years. The average yearly benefit is about $20,000—so most people also save money another way for retirement.

Paying for Medicare

Medicare is the health insurance program run by the US government. People who are 65 years and older can claim Medicare benefits. Those who are younger and suffer certain illnesses and disabilities may also be eligible for Medicare. In the same way as your Social Security comes off your paycheck, so too does your Medicare contribution.

The Medicare program doesn't cover all medical expenses for those over 65. For that reason, many people buy additional medical insurance from private companies.

Mastering Money

Each time you're paid, you'll get a pay stub—either on paper or online. A pay stub shows how much you earned and what was taken off, including taxes, Social Security, and Medicare. Always check your stub carefully. A small mistake, like the wrong Social Security Number, can cause big problems later on. This is what a pay stub looks like:

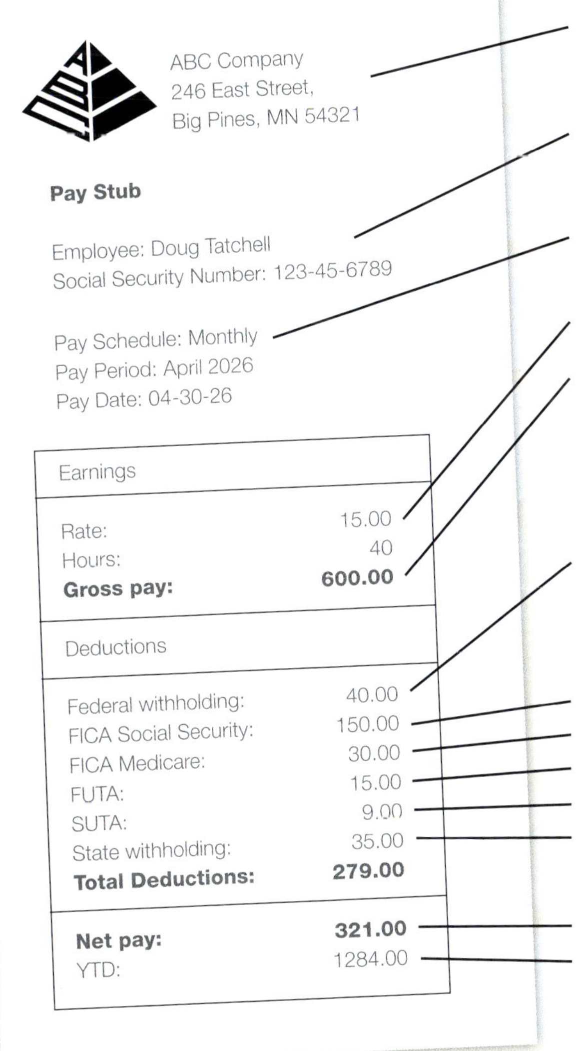

ABC Company
246 East Street,
Big Pines, MN 54321

Pay Stub

Employee: Doug Tatchell
Social Security Number: 123-45-6789

Pay Schedule: Monthly
Pay Period: April 2026
Pay Date: 04-30-26

Earnings	
Rate:	15.00
Hours:	40
Gross pay:	**600.00**

Deductions	
Federal withholding:	40.00
FICA Social Security:	150.00
FICA Medicare:	30.00
FUTA:	15.00
SUTA:	9.00
State withholding:	35.00
Total Deductions:	**279.00**
Net pay:	**321.00**
YTD:	1284.00

your employer's details

your details

how often you're paid

your hourly rate

what you earned before deductions

this is what the Federal government is deducting as a result of what you filled out on your W-4 form—see next page. Some pay stubs will have an additional column for what the state is withholding

what you pay into the Social Security fund

what you pay into the Medicare fund

stands for Federal Unemployment Tax Act

stands for State Unemployment Tax Act

this is state tax

what you take home after deductions

YTD stands for year to date and is what you've earned so far

Get Financially Fit:

Pay Taxes like a Pro

Expert Tips!

You've worked hard, earned money, and understand a little bit more about what taxes are. But how do you figure out if you need to file a tax return? And how do you calculate how much tax you're likely to owe the IRS? The two things that determine whether you need to file a return are your dependency status and whether or not you've earned over the income threshold. Here's some expert advice on how to figure out your tax situation.

What's Your Status?

Your dependency status is whether you are dependent or independent of your parents. If you are under the age of 19 (or 24 if still at school full time) and live with your parents for more than half of the year, you are still considered a dependent. Dependents then need to figure out how much they earned and if it's over the threshold. Everyone who is independent must file a tax return.

Filling in Forms

When you start a job, your employer will ask you to fill in a Form W-4. This form is called the Employee's Withholding Certificate. It's used to figure out how much federal income tax you will need to pay. However, if you fill out this form incorrectly, you could over or under pay. That's why it's important to do it carefully and get help if needed.

Take your time when filling out tax returns. It's important to get the details right.

Each time you start a different job, you need to fill in a new W-4. If you filled in a W-4, you'll get a W-2 form from each employer, usually in January. This form shows what you've earned for the tax year. If you're self-employed or have investment income, you need to fill in a Form 1099 to show your income.

Get It Together

If you know now that you need to file a return, you need to be very organized. Make a note of your Social Security Number. Gather your W-2 forms and/or 1099s if you were self-employed or earned money from your investments. If you plan to claim any expenses, make sure you have the receipts you need.

File Your Return

Some states still offer paper returns but there is also software to file your return. In many cases, you can use the IRS Direct File, which is the IRS online tax filing system. You need to file your return by 15 April for your income earned the previous year—for example, you file your return by 15 April 2026 for the money you earned throughout 2025. You'll need to work through the process step by step:

- Fill in your personal information.
- Report your income—use your W-2s for this.
- Choose your deductions, if any.
- Check for tax credits—there's more about this on page 30.
- Sign and submit the form.

You will need to keep any tax records for at least three years from the date of filing.

Getting a tax refund is a reason to celebrate! Instead of spending it right away, think about saving or investing it for the future. You'll find tips later in the book.

What Are Tax Credits?

Tax credits are money you take off what you owe the IRS. Tax credits work by first reducing your tax bill to zero. If the money you owe is zero and you still have a credit, that money is refunded by the IRS. The credit most likely to affect you now is the one for low earnings. For adults, credits will depend on their situation—whether they're married or have children. For example, an adult with a child under 17 may get a credit if the child has a Social Security Number and is listed as a dependent on the tax return. Some health insurance purchases also come with a credit.

Understanding Refunds

After you send in your tax return, the IRS reviews it. If you file online, it may take up to 72 hours to hear back. If you file by mail, it can take a month. If you're owed a refund, you can call the Refund Hotline to check its status. Once approved, the money will be sent to you.

Owing Money

If you owe tax, you must pay it by April 15. You can pay online by bank account or card. If you can't pay the full amount, you'll need to request a payment plan from the IRS. Even with a plan, you'll still get penalties and interest until the full amount is paid. That's why it's smart to save a little each month in case you get a tax bill.

Teens and Money

Sometimes teens feel upset after seeing how much tax they've paid. That money could've gone toward fun stuff! But remember—everyone who earns above the threshold pays taxes, and most adults pay even more. Taxes help pay for schools, firefighters, police, and people in need. Every taxpayer plays a part in making the country work. Your contribution matters.

Budget smart! Make sure you account for a potential tax bill when you plan your budget so that you can pay the IRS any money you owe at the end of the tax year rather than through a payment plan.

Paying Taxes Made Easy

We looked at a lot in chapter 3, and tax can seem complicated. But it's easy to manage once you get to grips with it. Here is a round-up of what taxes are and how to pay them.

Add Sales Tax to the Price

Everyone, regardless of income, pays sales tax on taxable goods. The percentage people are expected to pay depends on the state the goods are sold in and the type of goods.

Deductions Off Your Wages

By law, employers are required to take income tax off your wages or salary. The more you earn, the higher your income tax bill will be. Other deductions to pay include Social Security and Medicare.

File Your Return on Time

Everyone's tax returns can be filed electronically, through apps, or by filling out forms. Whichever method you choose, you need to file your return on time. If you have to pay a tax bill, it needs to be paid by mid-April, otherwise, you could get a penalty. If you get tax credits, you may get a refund from the IRS.

Paying Taxes Is a Civic Duty

Taxes are the main source of income for a government. The money the government receives from taxes is used to fund things that benefit each citizen. These include fire and police services, schools, and much more.

CHAPTER 4

Earning in the Future

As you grow older, you'll naturally become more independent of your parents. You'll start doing more and more for yourself, and you may leave home to go to college or to work. The way you earn money and pay taxes will also change.

Finding a Job

If you decide to go straight into permanent employment from school, you'll need to think about what work you'd like to do and what work you're best suited to. Job hunting can take time, so it helps to be organized. Set aside time each day to look for vacancies. Use job boards such as LinkedIn and Career Builder to help you find openings. Talk to people you know—someone might hear about a job before it's posted. Then adjust your resumé as needed to fit the job, and apply. Keep a list of jobs you've applied for and any notes taken.

You may know someone in the field you're interested in, so don't be shy to ask for advice.

Some schools have career counselors who can help and guide teens with their career choices. They can also advise teens with regard to what to study to achieve their career goals.

Although you may have your heart set on something, don't limit yourself—keep your options open and be flexible. It can be very disheartening applying for jobs and being rejected, but not everyone who applies for a job can get it. There can only be one successful candidate. If you go to an interview, ask the recruiter for feedback afterward. You can learn from this and apply it going forward. Accepting feedback is a skill you will need later in your working life too.

Finding Part-Time Work

If you're still in school or college, a part-time job can help with spending or student loan costs. These jobs might include being a server at a diner or helping with office work. If you choose wisely, your job can help your future career. For example, if you want to be a nurse, working at a medical office gives you helpful experience. You'll also learn skills on the job that you won't get in school.

Mastering Money

You don't have to go to work—you can earn money from the comfort of your own desk. Remote working is becoming more popular because all you need is the right skillset, a computer, and an Internet connection. By working remotely, you'll save on transportation and travel time. In some cases, you'll also be able to choose your hours to fit in with your schedule. Remote jobs include being a virtual assistant or virtual customer service agent, designing, programming, or writing.

Taxes Will Increase!

By now you know that the more money you earn, the more taxes you'll pay. Once you have a full-time job, it's likely your income will go over the tax threshold. That means you'll pay more tax than you did as a teen. This change also affects your parents. If they listed you as a dependent on their tax return, they may lose some tax credits once you're no longer counted as one. There are also new types of taxes to think about—like property tax and estate tax. These may not apply now, but they're important to understand so you are educated for the future.

Big-Buy Taxes

Once you have a regular paycheck and your own place, you might want to buy a car—or even a home. These are big purchases, so many people borrow money from a bank to help pay for them. Remember, banks will charge you interest on any loans, so you'll need to factor this into your budget. You'll also need to plan for property tax. This tax is payable once or twice a year, depending on the state. For tax purposes, "property" includes homes and other structures. The amount that needs to be paid depends on the value of the property. It also varies depending on the city and state. Property tax helps pay for local services like water, sewer systems, road maintenance, and libraries.

One day, you may want to buy your own car. You may need to borrow money to do so, and pay back that money along with interest.

Whenever possible, it's better to buy local products. Imported items will have a tariff so will be much more expensive.

What Is Estate Tax?

Most teens won't deal with estate tax, but it's helpful to know what it is. When someone dies, their money and property becomes their estate. This is passed down to others, like family members. If the estate is worth more than a certain amount, a tax must be paid on it. In 2024, that federal limit was $13.61 million—so most people wouldn't need to pay it. However, some states have lower limits, so more people have to pay estate tax at the state level.

Mastering Money

When goods are brought in, or imported, from another country, the government levies a tariff on them. For example, if there is a tariff on vehicle imports, any cars brought in from another country would be subjected to the tariff—such as 5 percent of the value of the car. The tariff is paid by those importing the goods, and this is passed on to the customer. When it comes to shopping, try to buy locally produced items because they will be cheaper and your money will go further.

Being Tax Savvy

Taxes can take a big bite out of your money, so it's smart to plan ahead. Once you're earning a steady income, you should think about setting up both regular and tax-smart accounts.

Taxable Accounts

Taxable accounts are ones where you might have to pay tax on the money you earn. This includes brokerage accounts or individual investment accounts. A brokerage account is where you invest your money through a broker—someone who helps buy stocks, bonds, and other funds. The taxes you pay depend on how you make money.

If you earn interest, you're usually taxed at your usual income tax rate. If you get dividends (a share of profits from stocks), you'll pay tax on that, too. If you sell investments for more than you paid, you pay a tax called capital gains tax. The amount you'd pay depends on how long you had the investment for. The longer you had it, the lower the tax rate. However, taxable accounts are quite flexible. You can access your funds whenever you need them and you can add to them whenever you like.

It's in your best interests to be as up to date as possible when it comes to tax matters. Do your research so that you know what's best for you and your money.

Tax-Advantaged Accounts

Tax-advantaged accounts are special accounts with tax perks. They're made to help people save for big goals like retirement, healthcare, or college. Some accounts let you delay paying taxes. These are called tax-deferred accounts. You don't pay tax when you put money in, but you will when you take it out—usually in retirement. This also lowers your current income tax.

Other accounts are tax-exempt. That means you might not get a tax break now, but you won't pay taxes when you withdraw the money later. Some accounts are a mix—they offer benefits when you put money in and also offer them when you take money out.

Mastering Money

Setting up tax-savvy accounts takes financial know-how so it's good to seek the help of a financial advisor. Meeting with a financial advisor can help you choose the right path—but do your homework first. Learn the basics so you can follow the conversation. Don't feel rushed into making a quick decision. Take your time to think and do more research. The choices you make now will shape your future.

Setting up different accounts can be confusing and one solution does not suit everyone. To make the most of your income, try to see a financial advisor. You will have to pay for your appointment, but it will be money well spent.

Get Financially Fit:

Invest like a Pro

Expert Tips!

As you earn more and more money, you'll need to learn to invest it wisely so that it can grow as you age. There are several short-term options, such as high-interest bank accounts. However, long term investments generally have better results. Here are some expert tips to steer you in the right direction when it comes to long-term investments.

Go for Compound Interest

A regular savings account is great as a teen. When you get to your 20s, it's a good idea to open a bank account that offers you compound interest. Compound interest is interest on the original money you invest *and* on what you earn, so interest on your interest. Depending on the bank account, interest can be added daily, monthly, every few months, or once a year. The longer you leave your money in an account with a good interest rate, the more it will grow over time.

Get into Real Estate

Property is a great way to invest your money. You might live in the home now, but later you could rent it out and earn income from tenants. Over time, property usually grows in value, which means you could sell it later for more than you paid.

Buy Savings Bonds

The US government offers savings bonds to raise money. When you buy a bond, it's like lending money to the government. They sell the bond for less than its full value, and after a certain time—usually 15 to 30 years—they pay you the full amount. You earn interest while the bond grows in value. This interest isn't taxed right away, but you may pay federal tax when the bond is cashed in. The good news is that state and local taxes do not apply to savings bond interest.

Plan for Retirement

Retirement may seem far off, but the sooner you plan for it the better. Individual Retirement Accounts (IRAs) are tax-advantaged saving accounts to help you when you retire. IRAs are a good choice for people who are self-employed or don't get a retirement plan at work. But you can also have an IRA even if you already have a job-based retirement account. IRAs allow you to invest in different products, from stocks and bonds to mutual funds. Simply put, you invest the money and wait until retirement to withdraw it. If you withdraw the money before retirement, you'll face hefty penalties as well as tax on the money you withdraw. So, you need to plan to keep the money invested until you stop working.

Retirement may seem like something only your grandparents need to think about! But it's always a good idea for young people to have a plan in place for when the time comes.

Sit with a parent or financial advisor to get started with your financial plan for the year.

Plan Ahead for Financial Freedom

If you want to be fully financially independent, you'll need a sound plan. A financial plan helps you understand what money you have, what your goals are, and how you can reach them. It also helps you manage your money better. To start your plan, use the tips in this book and some smart budgeting habits. Update your plan each year to make sure you reach your goals.

Set a Goal and Track Money

You can't create a plan without financial goals. Make a note of your short-term and long-term goals. If need be, revisit pages 40–41 for a long-term investment recap.

Next, make a list of all the money coming in—your income. Check your pay stub and write down your take home wage or salary. Write down your expenses. A good way to do this is to check your bank statement each month and make a note of what you're spending money on. Know what's left in your account at the end of the month.

Emergencies and Debt

Life is full of surprises. Try to save a little money each month, just in case. Even small savings can add up and keep you from going into debt when something unexpected happens. And if you do have debt, know exactly what you're paying and when the payments will stop. Try to avoid overspending on credit cards and make sure you only spend what you can pay off in one go.

Look to the Future

Write down your investments and where they should be in 5, 10, and 20 years' time. With the help of a financial advisor, keep tracking them to see how they are doing. It may seem silly as a teen to plan for something 50 years away, but it's important. The longer you have to save for retirement the better.

Tax Matters

You know now that taxes can take a chunk of your income so make a note of the taxes that come off your pay stub. See if you can be more tax efficient by setting up different accounts. Make sure that you have all your insurance needs thought through too.

Teens and Money

Studies show that younger people are 38 percent more likely to miss mortgage payments and 25 percent more likely to make withdrawals from their retirement accounts when things get tough. Anyone with a solid financial plan and budget will be better prepared and in control of their finances, and these slip-ups will be less likely to happen.

A spending spree is fun, but not if it's at the expense of a retirement or savings plan!

Future Earning and Taxes Made Easy

Some of the ideas in this chapter might feel tricky—but they will get easier to get a handle on over time. When it comes to money, the earlier you start planning, the better. Let's take a quick look back at what we've covered in this chapter.

Finding Work

Try to find a job in college that connects to what you're studying. It will give you real-world experience that classes can't always provide. If you're going straight into full-time work, finding the right job might take a while. It can be tough—but don't give up if things don't work out right away, Keep positive.

Taxes and More Taxes

As a young adult, you'll no longer be classified as a dependent so you'll likely need to pay more taxes than you did as a teen. It's important to pay your taxes, and you have to by law. But you can set up your finances to be as tax efficient as possible.

Invest What You Can

There are a lot of investment options and as a young adult, these should form part of your budget. You may not have a lot of spare money to invest, but if you start now, that money will grow as time goes by.

Plan Carefully

Setting out a financial plan is a good thing. Know what you have, what you want to have, and how you're going to get there. Talk through your financial plan with an advisor and revisit it at least once a year to help you stay on track.

You've learned all the skills you need to earn money, now make the most of it with great future planning.

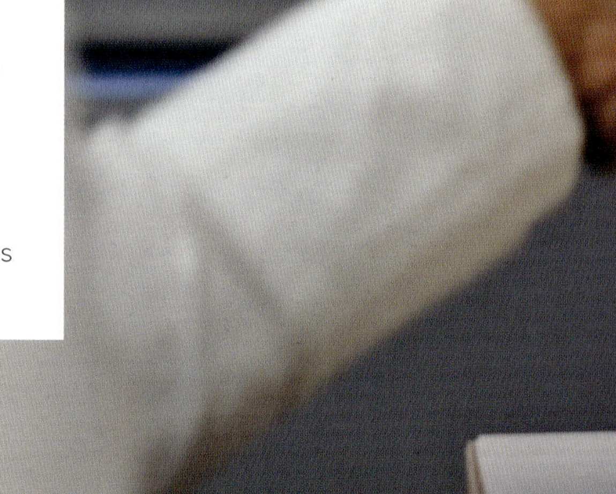

Glossary

allowance a sum of money paid regularly to a person to meet their needs
annually once a year or each year
anxious worried, nervous, or uneasy about something
benefits advantages gained
bonds types of loans
budget a financial plan that includes the income and expenses for a set period
contract a legally-binding written or spoken agreement
credit getting goods or services before payment on the trust that payment will be made in the future
debt money that is owed or due
dividends money paid regularly by a company out of its profits to its shareholders
employer a person or organization for whom others work
evaluating thinking carefully about something
exempt free from
expenses money needed to do or buy something
hazardous dangerous
income the money a person earns
insurance an arrangement by which a company promises to provide compensation for a specific loss, damage, illness or death, in return for a payment, which is called a premium
interest money paid regularly at a particular rate for money lent or earned
interpreting explaining the meaning of something
investing putting money into a financial scheme, shares, property, or business to make a profit
loan money that is lent to someone
manufacturing making something on a large scale
minimum wage the lowest amount of money a person can legally be paid to a person in exchange for their services
mortgage a legal agreement in which a bank or building society lends money to a person to buy property. The financial institution owns the property until the person pays off the loan
motivated wanting to do well or succeed
pension funds set aside for a worker's retirement
percentage a number expressed as a fraction of 100
profits differences between the money earned and spent in buying, operating, or producing something
retail the sale of goods or services
return the gain or loss on an investment over a specific period
risk possibility of a loss
seasonal fluctuating or being restricted according to the season or the time of year
self-employed working for oneself instead of an employer
self-reliant able to take care of oneself without outside help
service helping, assisting, or providing necessary tasks, support or actions to meet a need
siblings brothers and sisters
tenants people who pay a landlord rent

Find Out More

Books

Explore other *Money Matters* books to find out more about how to make your money work for you.

Eason, Sarah. *Budgeting* (Money Matters). Cheriton Children's Books, 2026.

Eason, Sarah. *Saving* (Money Matters). Cheriton Children's Books, 2026.

Sanderson, Jennifer. *Loans and Credit* (Money Matters). Cheriton Children's Books, 2026.

Websites

To find available jobs and learn more about them, take a look at the popular job search site "Indeed", at:
www.indeed.com

Visit the IRS site to find out everything you need to know about taxes, from filing a tax return to downloading relevant forms at:
www.irs.gov

Snagajob has so many great jobs to apply for. Log on at:
www.snagajob.com

Find out more about becoming an entrepreneur at the Young Entrepreneurs Academy:
www.youngentrepreneurs.academy

Publisher's note to educators and parents:
All the websites featured above have been carefully reviewed to ensure that they are suitable for students. However, many websites change often, and we cannot guarantee that a site's future contents will continue to meet our high standards of educational value. Please be advised that students should be closely monitored whenever they access the Internet.

Index

About the Author

Jennifer Sanderson has written books on many different topics, from sports and baby animals to geography and self-care. Jennifer has two teenage children who are learning how to navigate money matters and hopefully, like all teens, will learn the skills to understand how earning money and paying taxes will affect them as adults.

MONEY MATTERS

A Teen Guide to Earning Money

Money—it matters! You earn it. You spend it. But do you know how to make it work for you? From budgeting basics to beating debt, this smart series gives you the financial know-how you really need. Whether you're saving for something big, figuring out credit, starting your first job, or want to understand taxes, we've got you covered.

Jobs and Taxes

Making money feels great—but how can you earn it, and what are taxes? This book breaks it all down, showing you how to start earning, understand the tax you might need to pay, and use your income to build your future. Discover inside:

- Different ways to earn—now and in the future
- How to set up and run a business
- What tax is, why it matters, and how to handle it
- Top earning and tax tips from financial experts

Titles in this series

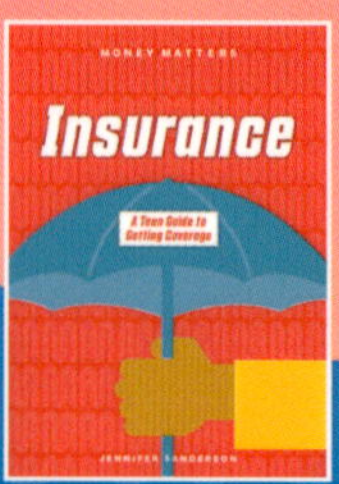

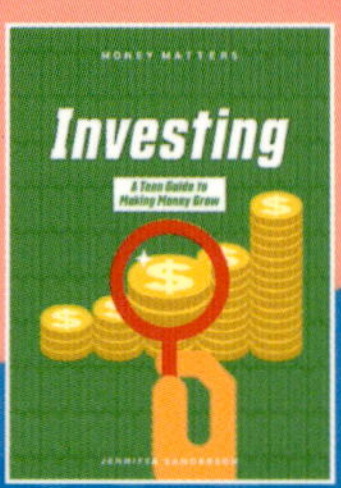

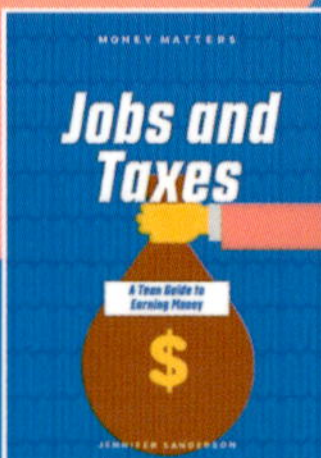

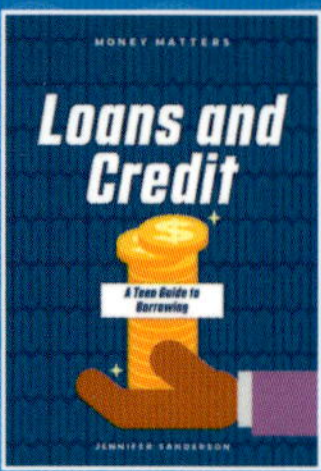

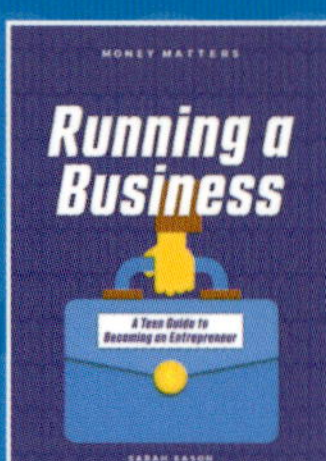

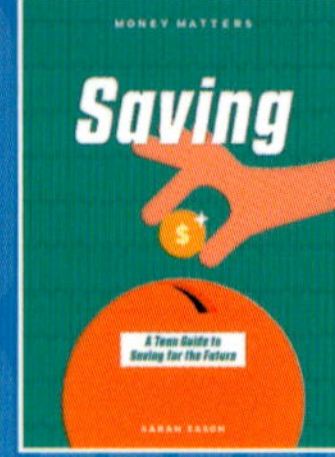